A Day in the Life of A Traffic Light

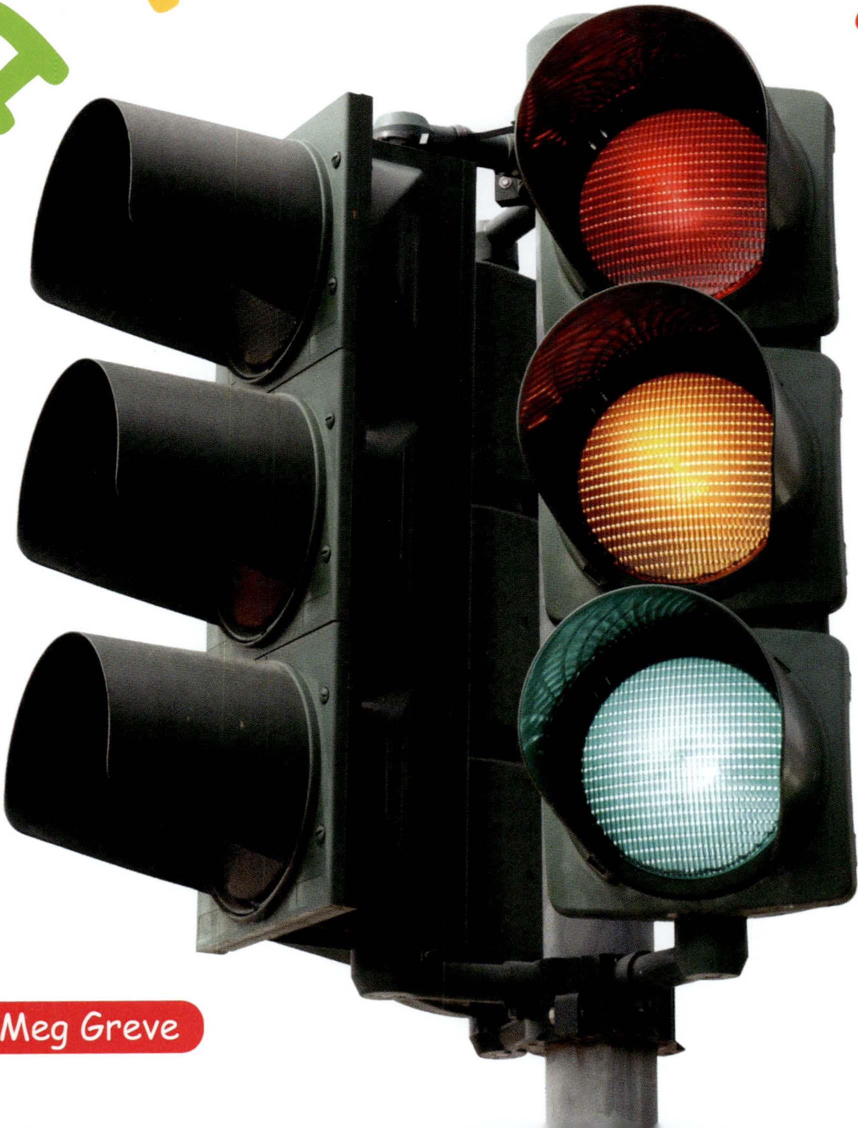

Meg Greve

EZ READERS
AN IMPRINT OF
MITCHELL LANE PUBLISHERS

CREATING YOUNG NONFICTION READERS

EZ Readers offer nonfiction for beginning readers in PreK through first grade, using simple language, clear illustrations, and engaging facts to build vocabulary and confidence.

TIPS FOR READING NONFICTION WITH BEGINNING READERS

Talk about Nonfiction

Begin by explaining that nonfiction books give us information that is true. The book will be organized around a specific topic or idea, and we may learn new facts through reading.

Look at the Parts

Most nonfiction books have helpful features. Our *EZ Readers* include color photographs and graphic aids, a table of contents, a glossary, and an index. Share the purpose of these features with your reader.

Color Photos and Graphic Aids

A lot of information can be found by "reading" photos, charts, maps, and other graphic aids found within nonfiction texts. Help your reader learn more about the different ways information can be displayed.

Table of Contents

Located at the front of the book, this list shows the big ideas within the text and the page numbers where they can be found.

Glossary

Located at the back of the book, the glossary defines key words and phrases that are related to the topic. These words and phrases can be found in the text in colored type.

Index

Located at the back of the book, an index is an alphabetical list of topics and the page numbers where they can be found.

With a little help and guidance about reading nonfiction, you can feel good about introducing a young reader to the world of *EZ Readers* nonfiction books.

EZ Readers is an imprint of:

Mitchell Lane
PUBLISHERS

2001 SW 31st Avenue
Hallandale, FL 33009
mitchelllanepub.com

First Edition, 2027.

Author: Meg Greve
Designer: Rhea Magaro
Editor: Kim Thompson

Library of Congress Cataloging-in-Publication Data
Title: A Day in the Life of a Traffic Light / by Meg Greve

Description: Hallandale, FL :
Mitchell Lane Publishers, [2027]

Identifiers:
ISBN 979-8-89260-847-3 (library bound)
ISBN 979-8-89260-937-1 (eBook)

Library of Congress Control Number: 2025950826

PHOTO CREDITS
Alamy: Keith Levit, 10; Richard Levine, 17; Dreamstime: Bumbleedee, 18, 22; Shutterstock: Blue Traffic Light, 1; Mega Pixel, 5; Veniamin Kraskov, 5, 22; ardiwebs, 7, 22; Here Now, 8; Pixel-Shot, 9; danielcgold, 13, 22; PaniYani, 14, 22; monticello, 21.

Table of Contents

I Am a Traffic Light

My top light is red. It tells **traffic** to stop!

My middle light is yellow. It means **caution**!

My bottom light is green. It means go!

Listen up!

I am in charge of this **intersection**.

I keep cars from crashing.

I keep **pedestrians** safe.

By THE WAY...
All must obey me!
I am not kidding.
(I would never joke
about safety.)

W 126 St
Sylvia P. Woods
Way
ONE
ONE WAY
DEPT OF TRANSPORTATION

I am green. Cars can go.

My DO NOT WALK **signal** is on. Walkers must wait!

BY THE WAY...

Wait at a **crosswalk**. Never cross in the middle of a street.

By the way...

Do not begin crossing before the WALK signal is on.

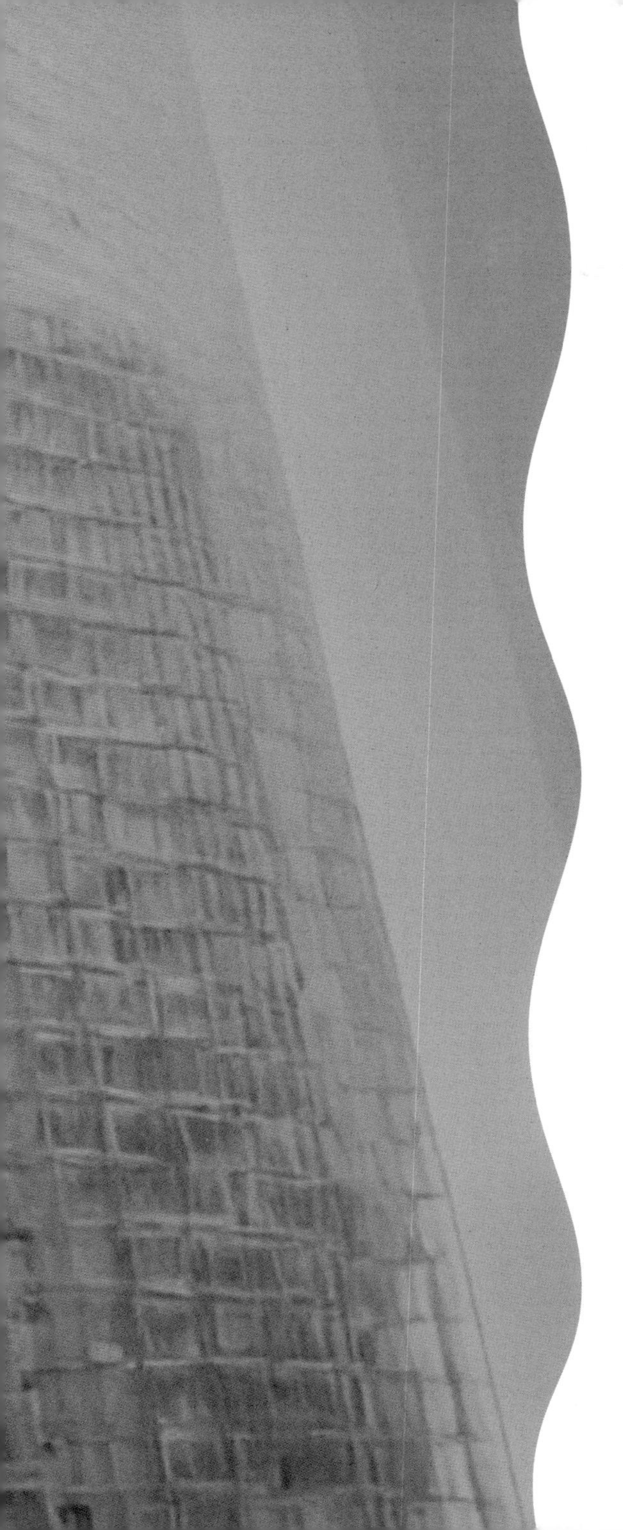

I am red. Cars must stop!

My WALK signal is on.
Walkers can go.

Be careful even when
I say WALK.

Look left, right, and left again.

By the Way...

Use your ears. You may hear car horns. You may hear **sirens**.

BY THE WAY...

Check that your shoes are tied. (Hey, I am just looking out for you, kid!)

Be alert as you cross.

Do not play. Do not look down.

My signal is flashing.

I will soon be green.

It will be the cars' turn to go.

Hurry up!

6

NYPD
NYPD
TRAFFIC
POLICE DEPARTMENT
CITY OF NEW YORK
NY

Sometimes, I stop working.

A police officer comes.

They **direct** traffic.

My job is important. (That is why I am so bossy!)

I keep everyone safe.

I will keep you safe too.

Glossary

caution (KAW-shuhn) a warning to be careful or watchful

crosswalk (KRAWS-wawk) a place where pedestrians can safely cross, often marked with painted lines

direct (duh-REKT) to tell people when and which way to go

intersection (IN-tur-sek-shuhn) the point at which two streets meet and cross each other

pedestrians (puh-DES-tree-uhnz) people traveling on foot; walkers

signal (SIG-nuhl) a sign or device that gives a message or warning

sirens (SYE-ruhnz) devices that make a loud sound to give a warning, often on emergency vehicles

traffic (TRAF-ik) all the moving vehicles on the road

Quiz Me

1. I only cross the street at a crosswalk.

   A. Yes B. No

2. I wait for the WALK signal before crossing.

   A. Yes B. No

3. I wait until cars are completely stopped before crossing the street.

   A. Yes B. No

4. I look left, right, and left again before crossing.

   A. Yes B. No

ANSWER KEY:

How many times did you answer yes?

4: Awesome! You know how to cross the street safely.

3: Great! You remember to think about safety.

2: That's okay! Keep learning and practicing.

1: You're starting to learn. Keep trying!

Further Reading

Day, William. *Kids' Safety Out and About.* Redback Publishing, 2025.

Lee, Maria. *Red Light, Green Light: Safe Street Crossing.* Epic Lotus, 2024.

On the Internet

Fun Kids: How Do Traffic Lights Work?
funkidslive.com/learn/roads/how-do-traffic-lights-work
Watch how a traffic light keeps everyone safe.

New York State Department of Health: Street Safe
youtube.com/watch?v=T5MI6DUPz6g
Learn how to safely cross the street.

Index

About the Author

Meg Greve has been in education for more than 30 years. She is a mom of two kids who learned quickly that red means stop and green means go. We like to take walks in our neighborhood and always look both ways before we cross, even when the signal says WALK!